Financial Independence – step by step to your own fortune
Independently published
©2020 Christoph Zimmermann
All rights reserved

Editing by: Liqui Finanz
Original version: ©2020 ETF – Von Ausführung bis Einkommen
Cover By: ©2021 Simboss Design

ISBN: 919-8589-89313-7

Financial Independence

Financial Independence

step by step to your own fortune

Christoph Zimmermann

Contents

Preface	9
The account model	10
The investment horizon	15
The four different types of investors	17
Definition of ETFs	19
The difference between distributing and accumulating ETFs	20
The difference between physically and synthetically replicating ETFs	21
The main stock indices of the world economy	23
The Risks of Exchange Traded Funds	27
The returns of ETFs	30
Find the right ETF	32
Choosing the right depot	36
Get to know sample portfolios	38
High Dividend Exchange Traded Funds	42
The dividend aristocrats	44

ETFs as a passive source of income   46

The most important terms in the stock market
                                        47

The bottom line about Exchange Traded
Funds   56

Disclaimer of liability   57

About the author   59

Preface

This book is intended to help readers who are interested in low-risk capital investments in the form of ETFs (Exchange Traded Funds) find the way to a passive income. In addition to the more complex topic of ETFs, the selection of custody accounts and fees is discussed, followed by explanations of the indices and various forms of ETFs.

At the end of the book, readers should be able to open a portfolio independently and with the necessary knowledge and create savings plans for ETFs.

If you do not yet have an account model for managing your finances, I strongly advise you to do so. Because only those who have a meticulous overview of their finances will experience the real joy of saving and building wealth.

The account model

Keeping an overview of your own finances can bring out one or two gray hairs. This includes both monthly fixed costs and any defects in important devices such as the PC for working, the car or planning a trip; after all, you want to enjoy life too. Fulfilling all of these points seems to be too much or even impossible for some people with only one account (usually the normal checking account). I will now show you, using a 5-account model, how you can get your finances under control.

For such a model to work properly at all, you have to understand the meaning behind it and have some discipline to adhere to it. In the best case scenario, you will even develop a joy in saving. You can also expand the various accounts as you wish. How many accounts there will be ultimately you decide how you think you best keep track of things.

First, you need to calculate your fixed and food costs and subtract them from your income. You use the remaining amount to service your other accounts on a percentage basis. This can look like this (the distribution should, however, be adjusted according to your needs):

- account for emergencies 30 %
- account for wishes 20 %
- investment account 25 %
- account of protection 25 %

The first account: Salary and all-round account

It is very likely that you already have the most important account: the current account. You not only receive your fixed salary on this account (this model also works in self-employment), but you also service all other accounts from here. Fixed costs such as rent, car insurance, livelihood etc. are debited from this account. For a better overview, however, it is advisable to keep an extra account for subsistence, to which you transfer a monthly fixed amount that you have determined in advance. Just keep in mind that not every account is free and there may be monthly fees. Here it makes sense to choose an account with a basic fee instead of transaction costs.

The second account: The emergency account

It is essential to keep an "emergency" account. Who does not know it, suddenly the refrigerator breaks down and has to be replaced quickly and in the following week your car won't start and has to go to the workshop. So that you are prepared for such incidents and do not have to fall back on your capital contributions (an absolute no-go, by the way), it is necessary to keep an "emergency account". For such an account, we recommend either a cash register at home or a call money account so that you can get your money as quickly as possible. It is advisable to limit this account with a certain amount. You determine this according to your requirements. If this limit is reached at any time, this sum is available to you monthly and you can move it to another account at your own discretion. The hedging account is recommended here first, or you can split the sum over several accounts. If the emergency account has to be looted, it is replenished monthly with the original amount until it can be capped.

The third account: account for wishes
As the name here suggests, the account of desires is solely for your pleasure. This account must not be underestimated, otherwise we quickly get the feeling that we have to do without it. As a result, we would lose our enjoyment of saving. Whether you want to save for a new car or perhaps a long-awaited trip is entirely up to you. Even small requests like going to a concert, buying new clothes or just going out with friends can be fulfilled with this account. Here, too, we recommend a call money account or a credit card for spontaneous requests.

The fourth account: pensions and investments
For this "account" you first need a deposit. There is also a free credit account, which will also be your deposit clearing account. Here, too, it is advisable to transfer a certain percentage of your net income to this account every month. Or you can have the savings plans debited from your reference account (account no. 1) by direct debit.

The fifth account: the insurance account
In some economic situations or in special cases such as a pandemic like in 2020, you can lose your job unexpectedly. Nothing is worse and more overwhelming than the ignorance of not being able to pay the running fixed costs. That is why the "safety account" is so important. As with the other accounts, you transfer a certain percentage every month until you have reached your self-determined limit. The limit should be so high that you can cover all costs with it for at least three - better up to six months. If you have reached this limit, you can split the monthly payment into one or more other accounts. Here, too, it is advisable to have a call money account in order to have quick access to money in the worst-case scenario.

THE INVESTMENT HORIZON

The investment horizon describes how long you want to invest your capital. Basically, this can be divided into three levels; short, medium and long term. The choice of the investment horizon depends on your personal investment goals.

Short-term investments usually do not go beyond the 24-month investment period. Here, liquidity has the highest priority. The typical short-term investment consists of a savings book or a daily or fixed deposit account. Short-term investments in certain stocks are also possible, but you should calculate this option in advance, as fees can result in small losses when buying or selling.

Medium-term investments usually have a term of 24 months up to six years. With such an investment horizon, the mix of security, liquidity and return is the decisive criterion. Fixed-term deposit accounts, time-limited bonds or various types of securities with dividend payments are possible for the medium-term investment variant.

The **long-term** investment horizon starts at six years. This type of investment is primarily used to build up wealth. Security and liquidity tend to take a back seat here. When it comes to wealth building, growth, high returns and broad diversification are the keys to success. Funds, real estate, ETFs or even certain stocks are the right financial products for a long-term investment horizon.

Which class of investment horizon you choose depends on your attitude towards risk and return. For some investors, a mix of investments can also be the key to financial happiness.

The four different types of investors

First of all, it is important to find out what type of investor you want to be. In order to determine this, you have to read through the following four descriptions of the investor types and determine for yourself which type you can best identify with.

The substance-oriented
The security of his investment and thus the preservation of his capital is very important to the value-oriented investor. For example, overnight money accounts and savings books play a role here, which guarantee returns in any case. However, it must be noted here that money is losing value due to inflation and the low returns of these investment methods often cannot compensate for this loss.

The profit-oriented one
The income-oriented investor can deal with any price and interest rate fluctuations, and yet the security of his investment has the highest priority. Investments are made, for example, in fixed-income securities or pension funds. Here, too, it can happen that inflation cannot be balanced out.

The growth-oriented
A growth-minded investor takes higher risks in order to achieve high returns. It is important to him that his investments increase. Investing in ETFs and stocks from companies with stable indices (e.g. the Dax or the NASDAQ-100).

The opportunity-oriented
As an opportunity-oriented investor, one wants to achieve the highest possible profits and returns and does not primarily focus on the security of an investment. A high degree of willingness to take risks is required in order to pursue speculations about price and currency fluctuations. Caution is required because the higher the profit expectation, the higher the risk of loss. Investments are made in individual stocks and ETFs. In addition, warrants and derivatives are traded in the hope of high profits - with a total risk of loss.

Definition of ETFs

The abbreviation ETF stands for Exchange Traded Fund and is an index fund traded on the stock exchange that tracks the value and price development of the respective index. An ETF can include shares of various companies as well as raw materials and real estate and thus ensures a broad diversification of the investment.

Compared to actively traded mutual funds, ETFs are up to a third cheaper, which has a positive effect on returns. Most ETFs have a TER (total expense rate) of 0.2 to 0.5 percent per annum and are deducted annually from the fund volume invested.

In the following, the differences between synthetic and physically replicating ETFs are explained and the advantages and disadvantages of distributing and accumulating ETFs are explained.

THE DIFFERENCE BETWEEN DISTRIBUTING AND ACCUMULATING ETFs

As mentioned in the previous chapter "What is an ETF", there are not only differences in the replication methods, but also in the receipt or processing of dividends. A distinction is made here between distributing and reinvesting ETFs.

Distributing ETFs
Distributing ETFs are those that pay investors their dividends at regular intervals. The period and intervals at which the distribution is made depends on the respective ETF and can happen quarterly, half-yearly or annually. In this case, the investor can decide for himself what should happen with the income he has gained. For the compound interest effect, the yields gained should be paid back into financial products.

Accumulating ETFs
In the case of an accumulating ETF, the income generated is automatically fed back into the ETF that has already been invested. As a result, there is no need to worry about reinvesting and investors automatically benefit from the compound interest effect and save the new order fee, which is charged by individual purchases depending on the broker.

THE DIFFERENCE BETWEEN PHYSICALLY AND SYNTHETICALLY REPLICATING ETFS

As mentioned in the previous part of the book, there are several types of replication methods, physical, synthetic, and optimized.

A **physical** ETF represents the full replication of an index. It reflects 100 percent the weighting of the shares in a smaller index such as the German share index (DAX), which lists only 30 of the most important German companies. With some indexes (e.g. with a listing of more than 1000 companies) a full replication does not make sense and one speaks of a partial replication. In the case of partial replication, only those company shares are listed that best and most accurately reflect the index. Here one speaks of sampling. When sampling, it can happen that there are deviations from the index to be mapped, called *tracking error*.

A **synthetic** ETF (also called SWAP ETF) replicates the index by means of swaps between two partners, so-called derivatives. Investments are not made exclusively in the values of the index to be replicated, but the swap partner tries to replicate the index's performance as best as possible.

ETFs with **optimized** replication only buy the most important or most liquid stocks with the greatest impact on index performance. This replication method is also known as "physical sampling".

Advantages and disadvantages of the replication methods

The advantage of synthetic ETFs is that, unlike a physical ETF, the exact values of the index do not have to be acquired. This reduces the administrative effort. Synthetic replications are often cheaper.

A not inconsiderable disadvantage with synthetic replications is the inability to pay (insolvency) of the swap partner. If such a case occurs, the price of the ETF can and will plunge rapidly downwards. In such a situation, severe losses or even total loss can be expected.

This topic is dealt with in more detail in the chapter *The Risks of Exchange Traded Funds*.

THE MAIN STOCK INDICES OF THE WORLD ECONOMY

Investors who want to invest money in the form of ETFs with low risk and security should always choose a broad diversification in the form of. Watch out for stocks, bonds, commodities and real estate ETFs. This ETF structure can also be divided into regions. For investors who want to start small at first or for investors with a smaller budget in general, an ETF that tracks the "MSCI World" index is suitable.

The MSCI World Index

The USA makes up the largest part of this index with a share of more than 65%. This is followed by Japan with 8%, Great Britain with 5%, France and Switzerland with 3%. The MSCI World includes a total of 23 industrialized countries and contains more than 1,600 stocks.

The MSCI Emerging Markets

Here, the People's Republic of China forms the largest share with 34%. This is followed by South Korea and Taiwan with 12%, South Korea with 9% and India with 7%. This index includes 26 emerging countries with more than 1,400 stocks.

Anyone who creates these two indices in combination invests and benefits from the entire global economy.

The S&P 500
This index lists 500 of the largest listed US companies. The S&P 500 is one of the most highly regarded stock indices in the world. It reflects the performance of the listed companies and is therefore an indicator of the development of the entire US stock market.

The STOXX Europe 600
This index reflects the 600 largest European companies. Among all European indices, the STOXX Europe 600 has developed into one of the reference indices in Europe. It is not only restricted to the European zone, because countries such as Switzerland and the United Kingdom are listed in this index.

The Nikkei 225
The Nikkei 225 is the leading Japanese index and therefore the most important and important index in Asia. As the name suggests, this index lists the 225 largest companies in the Japanese region.

The NASDAQ-100

Investors with an increased interest in technology should keep an eye on the NASDAQ 100. This price index lists 100 stocks with an increased share in the technology sector. Therefore, this index is also considered the technology index of the United States. The American financial sector is not represented in this index.

THE RISKS OF EXCHANGE TRADED FUNDS

Although investments in ETFs are considered low-risk, they still remain a financial product that can also pose certain risks for investors. These risks are discussed in more detail in this chapter.

The market risk
Although ETFs already form a diversification thanks to their wide range, there is still a certain market risk. Economic change - brought about by natural disasters, political differences or the economic situation - affects the indices and thus also the ETF based on them.

The exchange rate risk
Not every ETF is offered in the same currency. An example is the currency of the S&P 500, which is quoted in US dollars, the STOXX Europe 600 in euros and the Nikkei 225 in yen. Now the fluctuations in buying and selling the exchange rate must be taken into account. Here is an example: If you sell an ETF in a phase in which the US dollar exchange rate is weaker than when it was bought, the price discounts affect the return.

The risk of tracking error
As already explained earlier in the book, with physical ETFs there may be certain deviations from the index designed for them. This is exactly where the risks arise: The deviations can arise as yield deficits due to the management fees of an ETF. Delayed buying and selling of shares by the ETF operator can also cause deviations. This is referred to as the so-called tracking error or risk of deviation. The bottom line is that the greater the tracking error and the deviation it brings with it, the greater the resulting deficits in returns.

The risk with SWAP ETFs
In the case of synthetic or SWAP ETFs, the indices are made through swap transactions with the SWAP partner or the financial institution. Counterparty risk can arise with such ETFs. A synthetically replicating ETF depends on the SWAP partner always fulfilling its obligations towards investors. However, if this SWAP partner or the financial institution files for bankruptcy, the price of the associated ETF falls and the investors' money is no longer available. In order to counteract this risk, many ETF providers demand a certain degree of security from the respective SWAP partner, which significantly exceeds the actual value of the SWAP.

However, since there are no fixed rules for such collateral and this is not anchored anywhere, the investor should be aware of his investment in such an ETF.

The lump risk
Imagine you have just been shopping and you have all your purchases tucked away in a paper bag. What you unfortunately did not notice on the way from the car to the front door was that the milk bag broke on the way and the leaked milk soaked the paper bag. Shortly before the front door, the bag finally tears and all your shopping falls to the ground. However, if you had divided your purchase into several bags, only part of your purchase would now go to the garbage can. If you had divided your shopping into even more bags and other containers, a much smaller part of your shopping would have been broken.

It is exactly the same on the stock exchange: Avoid clumping by investing your entire capital in just one security, even if it beckons with the greatest returns. Spread the investments in different stocks from different companies - in different industries. In a simpler way, this would also be possible in individual ETFs, since an index inherently spreads further.

The returns of ETFs

Investing in ETFs is a comparatively safe and at the same time passive type of investment. Here, the investor himself decides on an index that the ETF should replicate. The investment is passive because there is no active fund manager behind an ETF, unlike actively traded investment funds, as the name suggests. With actively traded funds, the fund manager tries to generate a return by buying and selling stocks. This incurs higher costs for the investor, as the fund manager wants to be remunerated accordingly for his work. These costs will reduce the investor's return over the course of the investment period.

Exchange-traded funds have the advantage that they are not run by an active manager, which significantly reduces the costs of such an ETF. The following example shows the relationship between the costs of active and passive funds.

For the example we choose a deposit of € 25,000 over a period of 30 years. The monthly savings rate is € 500. The return for both types is 5% p.a. (per annum, per year). The total expense ratio is identified as TER (Total Expense Ratio).

*	active fund	passive fund
initial investment	25.000 €	25.000 €
monthly savings rate	500 €	500 €
return per year	5%	5%
Subscription fee	4%	0,4%
Total Expense Ratio	2%	0,5%
Investment period	30 Jahre	30 Jahre
Pure investment	205.000 €	205.000 €
Total profit after deducting total costs	332.683,81 €	464.481,65 €
Difference in the final amount		+ 131.797,84 €

This simplified calculation shows how the costs and fees of actively managed funds compared to passive ETFs reduce our return.

All values are only used for the simplified calculation.

Find the right ETF

First of all, it must be clear that there is no such thing as one perfect ETF. Not only the immense selection of different ETF products, but also the various details that an ETF brings with it can cloud the objective view. A good ETF is characterized by the fact that it suits the investor and his goals. Nevertheless, it is recommended to consider a few criteria. This chapter deals with the most important criteria.

The choice of indices
If the investor has decided on a region or industry (stocks, commodities, real estate or bonds), the choice of the index to be mapped is up. The broader an index, the better the value and risk diversification. With one of the broadest diversification, the MSCI World Index offers the greatest investment advantages. The more regional the index, the more indices should be added to the portfolio. For example, if the DAX, with only 30 of the largest listed German companies, is too centered, you should take a look at the STOXX Europe 50 or the even more widely diversified STOXX Europe 600.

The total expense ratio (TER)
The Total Expense Ratio (TER for short) is one of the most important criteria, as it can considerably reduce the return in the long term. The total cost ratio reflects part of the annual costs incurred by the provider and deducted annually from your invested fund volume. In addition, there are costs that are not included in the total cost ratio, such as Order fees for savings orders. However, these fees are shown at the financial institution where you have your custody account.

The fund age
The longer an ETF has been on the market, the greater the total fund volume and the better the ETF was introduced to the market. The age of an ETF therefore plays a role that should not be underestimated. An age returns a lot of information, such as the annual development or the amount and frequency of dividend payments. This makes it easier to compare an older ETF with the financial products of competing ETF providers.

The fund volume
Another important indicator besides the age of the fund is the fund volume. Experts consider funds with a volume of less than EUR 100 million to be unsafe. The advantage of a large fund is that the total expense ratio is usually lower.

The provider
The steadily growing market shows that ETFs are becoming more and more popular. This means competitive pressure for the providers and thus lowers the general total expense ratio. The largest and most popular providers are iShares, Lyxor, UBS, Amundi, Vanguard and ComStage. Most depot operations can be searched explicitly for these providers. However, caution is advised: some online brokers only offer savings plans for certain providers. This should be taken into account when choosing the broker and depot.

The performance
The performance shows us how "productive" an ETF really is and is made up of several factors. The development should be viewed from year to year, as ETFs, just like the indices on them, are exposed to economic fluctuations.

The ETF savings plan
If you want to build up your wealth continuously but step by step, you cannot avoid an ETF savings plan. With just a few ETFs in a portfolio, investors can already achieve a high level of diversification, which then do their part to build up their wealth by saving monthly. However, not every ETF is able to plan savings with every broker. Most ETFs capable of saving plans can be found at direct banks such as "comdirect".

Choosing the right depot

In order to be able to trade securities, ETFs or bonds and certificates at all, a deposit is required. This is carried out parallel to the current account. Either at the house bank or at one of numerous direct banks. First of all, the costs of a depot must be assessed. Most direct banks do not charge any custody account fees. Nevertheless, fees are to be expected even with such banks. Order, limit or fund fees are just a few items on the list of costs that may arise.

Order fees apply to the purchase or savings plan order of securities or ETFs. In the case of a direct purchase, this amount consists of a fixed fee; in the case of a savings plan order, the fee is a fixed percentage of the savings amount.

Limit fees arise when placing order limits.

Fund fees or management fees are incurred once a year and are deducted from the fund volume already invested.

There are various lists of direct banks and their savings plan-enabled ETFs on the Internet. If an investor is not sure in advance which ETFs should be saved, a direct bank with many ETFs capable of saving is the better choice. With a few online brokers, ETFs can be saved with low amounts and are therefore the better choice for investors with a shorter investment horizon.

Get to know sample portfolios

Sample portfolios are useful and serve as inspiration and support for new investors. The factors such as risk distribution, weighting of the industries and strategies for a targeted investment were taken into account when creating such model portfolios. Some of these portfolios are now given as examples. A large selection of such sample portfolios can be found on sites like **www.justetf.com**.

World stocks and emerging markets
This portfolio invests in stocks from developed and emerging countries around the world. It consists of only two ETFs and is therefore an interesting form of investment for newcomers to investors. You only have to pay attention to the weighting of the ETFs in order to ensure risk diversification.

1. MSCI World - 75 %
2. MSCI Emerging Market – 25 %

World portfolio 30

This model portfolio invests 30% in stocks worldwide and 70% in European government bonds. The indices of the industrialized and emerging countries are also used in this portfolio. There is also a bond ETF.

1. MSCI World – 20 %
2. MSCI Emerging Market – 10 %
3. Government bond ETF – 70 %

Gerd Kommer Strategy 2018

According to Kommer, the entire portfolio of an investor consists of a "risk-free" and a risk-prone part. The selection of ETFs is the same as for the world portfolio 30, however, due to a different weighting, it is much less risky.

1. MSCI World – 50 %
2. MSCI World – 20 %
3. Government bond ETF – 30 %

Sustainability ESG Screened Global BIP
This portfolio invests exclusively in "ESG-Screened" index stocks. This allows investors to participate in the profits of the stock market without investing in ethically questionable companies.

1. Index Equity Global Low Carbon – 60 %
2. MSCI Emerging Markets Socially Responsible – 40 %

justETF dividends 50
"With this balanced sample portfolio of 50 percent global stocks and 50 percent European government and corporate bonds, you are investing in the most reliable, dividend-paying companies such as Danone, Coca-Cola and McDonald's worldwide." Source: **www.justetf.com**

1. Equity fund from Europe - 10%
2. Asia-Pacific Equity Fund - 20%
3. UK equity fund - 5%
4. United States equity fund - 15%
5. Government bond fund Europe - 35%
6. Corporate bond fund Europe - 15%

The ARERO world strategy (for experts)

This portfolio follows a long-term investment strategy. The diversification results from the division into equity, bond and commodity funds. "You can also use the ARERO strategy via a public fund (ISIN: LU0360863863) from DWS Invest-ments S.A. invest. This is particularly cost-effective for savings plans and investment amounts below 10,000 euros. The running costs as of May 31, 2020 were 0.50 percent per year (excluding the issue surcharge). This ARERO world fund carries out scheduled rebalancing, the so-called reweighting, twice a year. On the fifth business day in May and November, the asset classes are reset to their original proportions. "Source: **www.justetf.com**

1. Equity fund from Europe - 15%
2. MSCI Emerging Market - 25%
3. Asia-Pacific Equity Fund - 5%
4. United States equity fund - 15%
5. Government bond fund Europe - 25%
6. Raw material fund - 15%

High Dividend Exchange Traded Funds

What exactly is a dividend? Dividends or returns are the portion of a company's profit that is distributed to shareholders as a percentage. The amount of the dividend is decided at the annual general meeting and is based on the company's annual profit. ETFs with a high dividend strategy map an index that consists exclusively of companies with high yield distributions.

The 5 most important dividend indices

The **EURO STOXX Select Dividend 30** Index lists 30 of the highest dividend companies in the Eurozone.

The **S&P High Yield Dividend Aristocrat** Index lists the 60 companies with the highest dividends in the S&P 1500 Index.

The **UK Dividend** Index lists the 50 highest dividend companies in the United Kingdoms.

The **DivDAX** lists the 15 companies of the DAX with the highest dividends.

The **STOXX Global Select Dividend 100** Index lists the 100 companies with the highest dividends from the STOXX Global 1800 Index. The most important dividing indices are listed:

Index	dividend
FSE DIVDAX PR EUR	5,42 %
STOXX Global Select	6,71 %
S&P Global Dividend	6,96 %
FTSE UK Dividend Plus	12,34 %
EURO STOXX Select	7,14 %

Source: https://de.extraetf.com/ratgeber/investieren-in-dividenden-etfs

THE DIVIDEND ARISTOCRATS

Individual examples of dividend aristocrats include companies like Johnson & Johnson, Coca-Cola, Siemens, and Philip Morris. The shares of such companies ensure that the distribution of dividends increases year after year. The term aristocrat is only used when companies have consistently raised dividends for over 25 years. The best dividend payers come from down-to-earth industries and operate a company in the utility, industrial, retail, banking or real estate sectors. There are many ETFs on the market that only track indices with dividend aristocrats.

The 5 biggest dividend aristocrat ETFs

Vanguard FTSE All World High Dividend Yield
3,40 %

iShares STOXX Global Select Dividend 100
4,15 %

SPDR S&P Global Dividend Aristocrat
3,70 %

Xtrackers STOXX Global Selected Dividend 100
4,98 %

Lyxor SG Global Quality Income NTR
4,58 %

Source:
https://www.justetf.com/de/news/musterportfolio/dividendenaristokrats-ertragreiches-dividenden-portfolio-einfach-mit-etfs-umsetzen.html

More regional dividend aristocratic ETFs

SPDR S&P Euro Dividend Aristocrat   2,98 %

SPDR S&P US Dividend Aristocrat   1,67 %

SPDR S&P UK Dividend Aristocrat   2,91 %

SPDR S&P Pan Asia Dividend Aristocrat   2,85 %

ETFs AS A PASSIVE SOURCE OF INCOME

ETFs with high dividend payouts are ideal as an additional source of income with the "monthly dividend strategy". By choosing the right ETFs, it is even possible to distribute dividends monthly. Attention must be paid to the quarterly distribution and the staggered arrangement of the funds. If one ETF pays the dividends in January, April, July and October, the next ETF has to pay out in February, May, August and November. Then you still need an ETF for the remaining months of March, June, September and December. This means that you can increase your monthly income by permanently saving just three ETFs. The following pages are recommended as a source of information to help you find the right ETFs:

www.justetf.com

www.extraetf.com

THE MOST IMPORTANT TERMS IN THE STOCK MARKET

Active and passive investment
After reading this book, it is understandable that ETFs are passive investments. However, the actively managed funds have also been around for some time. These are managed by fund managers, whose aim is to outperform the index to be tracked in order to achieve an even greater return. Actively managed funds have much higher fees, which ultimately reduce the return by a significant amount. This type of fund should only be used if there is no passive alternative for the index to be tracked.

Asset classes
The asset class is directly related to risk appetite. The different types of system types have already been explained in the front part of the book. The classes are also divided into risk-averse and risk-averse groups.

Bonds
Bonds are debt securities that are taken out on the capital market through a loan. The difference to a privately taken out loan is that bonds are only issued publicly and only by legal entities. Bonds differ from conventional loans in terms of their length of term, currency and interest rate. The interest rate depends on certain events and differs in fixed, variable or structured returns.

Subscription fee
When buying or saving an ETF, the investor pays a front-end load. Either as a fixed fee or a percentage order fee and commission. These fees vary depending on the broker and financial product.

Benchmark
Benchmark is the name for a comparative value that is compared to a fund as an orientation. In the case of a fund, this is usually an index.

(Online) broker
The broker (in German: "Makler") is responsible as a service provider for the implementation of securities orders from investors. As is usually the case, the broker receives a commission or a commission for acting on behalf of the investor. A few brokers also offer advice and buy / sell recommendations.

Diversification
Diversification means spreading assets and investments across various investment objects.

Fundamental analysis
Company data, economic indicators and market analyzes are fundamental data and thus the most important attributes of a fundamental analysis. The intrinsic values of a security are determined in the form of a share.

Bid-ask spread
The bid-ask spread is the difference between the bid price (the price that investors are willing to buy) and the ask price (the price at which investors would sell). Usually the ask price exceeds the bid price.

Capital increase

The capital increase is the increase in the share capital of a company located on the stock exchange by issuing new, young shares. This procedure must first be approved by over 75% of the shareholders entitled to vote at the general meeting. The previous shareholders have the right to keep their percentage stake by buying new, young shares. In the event of a capital increase, the existing shareholders receive free or bonus shares.

Price-to-book value ratio (P/B)

The price / book value ratio is a substance-oriented key figure for assessing the value of shares. Here the price of an individual share is compared to its proportional book value. The formula for this is as follows:

P/B = price of a share / book value of a share

An example: According to the annual financial statements, a company has equity of EUR 300 million. The company has 15 million shares in circulation. This results in a book value of 15.00 euros per share. A current share price of EUR 13.50 divided by the previously determined value results in a P / B of 0.9.

One theory of value investing is that the lower the P / B, the cheaper a stock is. A good stock value is roughly equivalent to book value. More current valuation methods are instead based on the P / E ratio, price-earnings ratio.

Price-earnings ratio (P / E)
The price / earnings ratio is a frequently used indicator for assessing stocks. Here the price of a share is set in relation to the earnings per share determined or expected for a comparable period. Mostly, estimates are used for future profits.

P / E = price of a share / earnings of a share

An example: The current price of a share is 135.00 euros. In the previous financial year, a profit of EUR 8.00 per share was achieved. This results in:

P / E = 135/8 = 16.9

Since the 1990s the KG ratios have fluctuated from 12 (cheap) to 25 (expensive) in relation to the overall market.

Order

The buying and selling of securities is known as an order in technical jargon. The most commonly used order is the market order, in which purchases and sales are made at the current price. This is called an unlimited order.

Limit order is the name of an order with a fixed price and / or a fixed time frame for execution. For example, you want to buy company XY shares at a certain price, which is currently too expensive. With the limit order, you set your desired price for a limited or open period. As soon as the desired price of the share results, the pre-saved order is placed by your broker.

Market capitalization

Market capitalization is the arithmetical total value of the shares in a company listed on the stock exchange. It is calculated from the market value, the market price traded on the stock exchange and the number of shares in a company in circulation. Own stock is not taken into account when calculating market capitalization.

An example:

The number of shares issued (3,000,000 shares) minus the number of shares held (350,000 shares) results in the number of free shares in circulation (2,650,000 shares) multiplied by the current market price of each share (75 €.) then results in a market capitalization of 19,875,000 €

Performance fee
In addition to ongoing administration and management fees, many funds charge an additional performance fee, which is usually between 4% and 26%. This is to reward the fund manager's good work

Small, middle and large cap
In the case of shares, a distinction is made between different size classes. There are small and medium-sized companies as well as large corporations. In the stock exchange there are certain terms for such companies. "Small Caps" are small companies, "Middle Caps" are medium-sized companies and "Large Caps" are large corporations.
Large caps, or "blue chips", are known to most people. These are the largest companies in the country. In the USA, Microsoft, Amazon and Apple are among the blue chips. In Germany it is companies like BMW, Deutsche Bank or Deutsche Telekom.

Large caps have advantages and disadvantages. Such large corporations are proving to be quite robust. Often they can withstand severe economic crises or - as is currently the case - global pandemics. If such a large corporation were in serious danger, the state would presumably do everything necessary to save it. But such large companies also have some disadvantages that should not be underestimated. Many of these corporations are experiencing something like a creeping erosion of their economic strength. Over many years, companies like these have developed their own characteristics and continue to move away from customers. In the end they often resemble clumsy administrations with overweight bureaucracy. Their ability to innovate often also suffers from their own size.

Administration fee
The ETF management fee is very low compared to actively managed funds and is between 0.05% and 0.75% annually. The fees are calculated proportionally for each day and automatically deducted from the fund's assets.

Volatility
Volatility is used to measure the fluctuation range of security prices, commodity prices, interest rates or even mutual fund bonds over a certain period of time.

WKN and ISIN
The securities identification number, or WKN for short, is a six-digit combination of numbers and letters used in Germany to identify securities.
The international securities identification number, or ISIN for short, is a twelve-digit combination of letters and numbers and, like the WKN, acts as an identifier on international stock exchanges. The first two letters of the ISIN indicate the home country of the security.

The bottom line about Exchange Traded Funds

The ETF market has grown rapidly in recent years, and not without reason. A characteristic and also very important point are the low running costs and the minimal expenditure of time.

This rather low-risk variant of the investment is particularly recommended for newbies who have decided to invest in securities.

Basically, however, you should research well in advance which type and industry you want to discuss, because ETFs are a long-term investment that can easily be held for> 30 years.

By mapping a certain index, investors should be aware that this index can and will suffer fluctuations. In such cases it literally means: wait and see and drink tea. Panic selling should be strictly avoided as such actions can result in losing money.

Conclusion:

Investors who research well in advance and can keep their nerves in the event of falling prices will find a long-term and also profitable investment in ETFs.

Disclaimer of liability

The author assumes no liability for risks and the possible loss of money. Every investor should be aware of the possible financial damage.

© 2021 Christoph Zimmermann

The work including all contents is protected by copyright. All rights reserved. Reprinting or reproduction (including extracts) in any form (print, photocopy or other processes) as well as saving, processing, copying and distribution using electronic systems of any kind, in whole or in part, is permitted without the express written permission of Publishing prohibited. All translation rights reserved.

The use of this book and the implementation of the information contained therein are expressly at your own risk. The publisher and the author cannot accept liability for any accidents and damage of any kind that occur when visiting the places listed in this book (e.g. due to a lack of safety information) for any legal reason. Legal and compensation claims are excluded. The work, including all content, was prepared with the greatest care. Nevertheless, misprints and incorrect information cannot be completely ruled out. The publisher and the author assume no liability for the topicality, correctness and completeness of the contents of the book, nor for printing errors. The publisher or author cannot accept any legal responsibility or liability in any form for incorrect information and the resulting consequences. The operators of the respective Internet pages are solely responsible for the content of the Internet pages printed in this book

List of sources under:
http://liquifinanz.de/quellenverzeichnis

ABOUT THE AUTHOR

My name is Christoph Zimmermann, I was born in 1988 and come from the Aachen district in North Rhine-Westphalia.

At the age of 20, I completed my training as a metal designer (art blacksmith) and started in my father's company at the time. I quickly developed a lot of new skills at the management level and in the financial management of a company.

After more than 10 years in this position, I realized that this was not the job I wanted to do until I retired. I decided to leave the company and looked for a job with new challenges so that I could acquire completely new skills. I quickly got a job in a local online shop with a focus on technology.

Today I still work full-time in this position, but at the same time I am building up my independence, with the aim of being able to make a good living from it in 7 years at the latest (when I have reached the age of 40).

I owe my way to the stock market and securities, in the truest sense of the word, to an accident. After a bicycle accident and a shattered collarbone, I felt handcuffed at home. I was not allowed to pursue my hobbies, cycling and strength training, for over 3 months. For a long time I have been toying with investing my money in securities and so I make good use of my illness time and during this time, almost day and night, I continued to educate myself on this topic. That I have a talent for numbers and mathematics became clear very early in my school days.

In fact, the bicycle accident was a wake-up call to escape the hamster wheel. A "tragedy" that got the stone rolling in my life.

Now in every free minute of my free time I work to help people who also have the need for financial freedom. An added value for everyone!

<u>I wish you a wonderful day and hope that you too can make your dreams come true!</u>

Sincerely

Christoph Zimmermann - Founder & CEO of Liqui Finanz

www.ingramcontent.com/pod-product-compliance
Lightning Source LLC
Chambersburg PA
CBHW070825220526
45466CB00002B/758